Musings of Immortality

If society is to change for the general good, there must be a radical change at the foundation of our political, economic, and social systems. First, nations must commit to disarmament; but since this is unfeasible given today's military-industrial complex and the way in which nations interact when it comes to the production and distribution of goods and services, each nation must choose between the status quo and a New World Order.

There must be a shift from inequality to equality. This means that all currencies must have the same value; and the way Nations trade must not be based on the stock market model. When nations trade they should do so according to the Marxian statement that [goods and services must be distributed] "from each according to his ability, to each according to his need." If nations fail to do this then their economies will always be plagued by poverty and inequality, and political conflict will always be on the horizon.

We must change the way we live and interact. We must change our thinking and the way we treat each other. In other words, we must build houses for the poor, clothe the needy, feed the hungry, empower the disadvantaged and dispossessed. Instead of erecting an army of killers and destroyers, we should set up an army of builders and providers.

We must change the way we populate our lands; we must change the way we procure our livelihoods; we must change the way we teach our children. In other words, our children should be raised by the world rather than just their immediate families; we must depopulate our cities so that the people can learn to live in harmony with the natural environment; we must stop letting our young blindly choose their careers, instead, young people should be allowed to choose their professions according to their own likes and dislikes; and society should provide such that no one is left illiterate, skill-less, or unemployed. That is not to say that everyone should be forced to work. Indeed, there will always be people who are partly or entirely dependent on society. What I am saying is that people should be chosen for work according to their aptitudes.

I look to the day when national leaders erase their borders with impunity; a day when all peoples speak the same language; a day when all peoples come together as one; a day when our population size ideally fits our economy; a day when all peoples are cosmopolitans; a day when Utopian Socialism supersedes capitalism; a day when we settle all of our differences; a day when populations are not reproducing helter-skelter, but in a way that keeps the human population at one or two billion; a day when no one is starving, homeless, or suffering from a preventable disease; a day when ordinary people do not have to steal, beg, or borrow; a day when everyone can live their lives to the fullest.

National leaders need to understand that people do not need more prisons, or another way to kill and subvert one another; people do not need lawyers, taxes, and equivocal politicians. People need altruistic leaders, monasteries, economically viable communities, and governments that actually care about them and the things that are in their best interest. They need to recognize what's wrong with society and redress those things.

I am not a politician. I am not an economist. And I am not an expert when it comes to population control. Notwithstanding, it is not hard to see that if populations keep on reproducing haphazardly, they will keep on increasing geometrically; or that if populations keep on reproducing wildly, the resources that these populations need will not be abundant forever, that these resources are finite, and that demand for these resources will eventually outstrip supply. Likewise, we need to realize that certain political ideologies are not consonant with the type of New World Order that I am trying to describe; namely, conservatism. What is conservatism? Conservatism means a lot of things. It means national, international, and global capitalism. It is anti-populist and anti-socialist. It is at best the strong exploiting the weak; at worst, reactionary-ism. Domestically, conservatism means defunding popular social programs such as Medicaid, Medicare, Social Security, etc. It means less regulation of business so that corporations can run rampant and do whatever they want. It means more taxes for the working class and tax cuts for the rich. It means subverting native populations by continuing the current immigration policies. Internationally, it means preying on weak, undeveloped nations. For example, when a popular leader like Argentina's Peron gets elected conservative leaders subvert and ultimately overthrow him and his aides. In this way Chile's Allende got removed from office by [of all people] the bloodthirsty Pinochet; Congo's Lumumba got overthrown by the opportunist Mbeka; and so on and so forth throughout the entire globe. You have to ask yourself: on what scale is this progress?

Why Things Are Thus

Leaders and ordinary people do not have to over-exert themselves intellectually to discern that something is wrong with the current system of things. Indeed, not even children misperceive the ambivalent nature of the world. What people fail to realize is that certain spiritual forces are struggling for their very souls, and this is why the world is the way it is. You see, the Gods are very keen on collecting their individual shares of the world's spirits. More succinctly, the Devil is struggling for his share and so is Jesus Christ. If the world was entirely righteous or holy the Devil wouldn't get his share, as these souls would intrinsically go to God. Likewise, if the world was entirely evil or wicked God wouldn't get his share, as these souls would intrinsically go to Satan. To be sure, God and Satan feed on the energies of the good and the evil, respectively. Spirits that emit positive energy to the universe supply holy Gods with energy; thus, the need to surrender that energy in the form of worship. Likewise, spirits that emit negative energy to the universe supply energy to evil entities; and surrender that energy in the act of worship. This is why the Gods insist on worship.

The question is: how does this situation affect human society? Evil Gods have a vested interest in keeping the world the way it is since immorality, wickedness, corruption, and et cetera keeps them supplied with a massive, constant flow of energy. If they ever gained full control of the planet they will be able to radically restructure the very foundations of society to the extent that all mundane energy would be negative and, thus, go to them. Holy Gods have a vested interest in preventing evil from reigning supreme on Earth, as they get their energy from people who exercise good morals, righteousness, justice, etc. So now you know why the world is thus.

Mental Culture

In reality, the souls of sentient beings on Earth are on the whole mired in ignorance. For them to free themselves of their benightedness they must learn to think for themselves and for others; they must develop their minds to the point of enlightenment. Once enlightenment is attained, reality will reveal itself. The question is: what is reality? The reality is that sentient beings are the focal point of a spiritual struggle between God and Satan for their hearts, minds, and souls. The problem is that the average person is not subtle enough to perceive when Satan and God are interacting with them much less the political, social, religious, and economic ramifications of the Gods' spiritual politics. This is because of the subtlety and perniciousness of the medium that the Gods utilize when they communicate with sentient beings from Earth. What is this "medium?" The medium is a nonmetallic, energetically self-sufficient (since this device gets its energy from the electrical impulses that our brains give off) skull implant which enables its controllers to telepathically communicate with people, control peoples' minds and bodies, and even see what they see with their eyes on a computer screen. To establish communication and interaction all the Gods and their managers have to do is tap (with a computer) into the wireless frequency of the device in a person's head. In this way humans are all under the joint control of God and Satan since this device vitiates free will and free thought. What's more, this device connects our minds to a super-computer called Big Brother and, hence, cyberspace. Our dreams are not mere subconscious phenomena that we considered during the day; they are instances where our souls are temporarily uploaded to cyberspace. To be sure, individuals can consciously (to do some work, e.g. to make a movie, song, or television commercial, for example, or to "remote view" or "remote control" or "remote influence" peoples' minds) enter cyberspace and subconsciously (when we fall asleep or when the managers "freeze" our minds and bodies) enter cyberspace. This implant also enables its controllers to review the entire history (both previous and current lives lived by the individual) of every sentient being that is in physical form on planet Earth. Indeed, this technology is so sophisticated that it enables its controllers and Big Brother to retrace every mental step one takes, which enables it to dig up almost every single detail of people's lives. This retracement feature also enables Big Brother and its managers to almost instantaneously mobilize entire populations for or against others. By far one of the most insidious features of this technology is the magical changing of text in literature and public ads so to subvert or communicate with the reader. I still am not sure how this is done, but I am sure that the movie "Matrix" elucidated this phenomenon. Indeed, most of what can be seen on television is based on fact. One merely has to have an open mind in order to discern the factual from the bullshit.

People who know about this technology usually do not know how long it's been in effect on mundane populations. Assuredly I say to you, this technology has been around much longer than the very lifespan of Jesus Christ.

If the Gods' felt you were not being your true self they simply incarnate or reincarnate you and delude you via said device. If one manages to break out of the shell which comprises his or her actual reality, they simply delete from your conscious memory whatever triggered your transformation via said device. So you see, we are all a part of the "Matrix!" this great "mental culture" which is at once national, international, global, interplanetary, and even (if my estimates are correct) inter-dimensional and inter-galactic.

The Yin-Yang System

What do I mean when I postulate that the Yin-Yang system is better than Pure Evil or Pure Good? There is no such thing as Pure Evil or Pure Good inasmuch as every living thing is an expression of the dichotomy of these two entities, which is why I say that the Yin-Yang system is superior to all others. What's more, just like the U.S. constitution, there must be checks and balances to individual power. Take the human mind for instance: it is made up primarily of three things—the id, the ego, and the superego. The id is where we get all of our evil impulses. The superego is where all of our good impulses come from. The ego is what balances the two.

If we take the mind for our example we see that it is wisest to have both evil and good in our spirituality and social system. This is sound so long as we balance the one with the other. Moreover, without the id we would lack the mental requirements that we need to survive in a physical environment. Without the superego we lack the requirements we need to make wise choices and decisions that lead to higher levels of thinking and being. So you see, the human mind is the microcosm; the universe is the macrocosm. Our minds reflect the very order of the cosmos!

P.S.: YOU'RE SNEAKY, BUT I'M SUBTLE; YOU'RE CLEVER, BUT I'M WISE; YOU'RE WICKED, BUT I'M CRUEL!!!

Poems

A still-life at night, by the noisy mango tree, touched by the glow of a lantern on the porch, illuminates this memory forever. (The sound of laughter) To give it feeling the people make each other happy, while the pouring rain drops all over the scene, wetting the petals of every flower.

As a ghost, unknown to the physical world, I pass through these bleak trails for eternity. This year a sad feeling passes through me as autumn winds sweep fallen leaves past my shadow-less form.

How to Rule

Before anyone can rule there must be no question as to his or her competence. Rulers must not be randomly chosen to rule; they must be handpicked and cultivated: some rulers are born to rule, while others are chosen according to the way their ideologies suit the issues and problems facing the government. In the case of the Honduran Government the political questions are plainly laid out, and so are the solutions. First of all, political power must be concentrated in the hands of the ruler. In effect, the ruler will rule by decree, provided that he or she is wise enough to successfully manage the affairs of the nation. If he or she is wise and prudent enough then let nothing become an obstacle to his or her policies. Let nothing impede the progress he makes. Let nothing or no one subvert or depose him.

This is all well and good. However, to ensure that nothing gets in the way of the ruler or ends his reign there must be both a national and international consensus among the peoples of the Third World and the Honduran nation. In the case where enemies abound nationally and internationally the ruler must, in the words of Machiavelli, "[learn] to be both fox and lion," and all relations with nations or nationals that try to subvert the ruler's hegemony must be severed immediately. In other words, if constituents are attempting to subvert the ruler he must identify, isolate, and defang them immediately. If the common people are agitating against him he must sagaciously handle the situation, even if this means showing them "tough love." If the legislative organ is obstructing him the ruler must quickly dissolve it. This is true of every other organ of government. If there can be no consensus then political freedom will not remain intact. This is how sedition must be dealt with.

As to the question of personal property let there be no misunderstanding as to what the ruler means; namely, that no individual should own land, businesses, utilities, transportation, or financial institutions. These things must be owned and controlled by the people. This is axiomatic since private property is a social bane. If the government needs a piece of land then the government should have the power to expropriate that land. If a business is not profitable or harms society then the government should have the power to shut down or alter that business.

If public institutions were in private hands the people would have to pay for their services, something I think the people should not have to do. Indeed, all property should be owned by the people in general. The people should not be taxed by the government. Instead, the people's needs must be provided for by the government, as the government is the father of the people; and the nation is the mother. If a person or couple needs a car or a home government industries should build it and give it to them free of charge (or at a very affordable price). But make sure that companies are not producing cars and homes willy-nilly, but in a way that guarantees each nuclear family a car or home. In this way, the capitalist creed that competition fosters economic productivity and efficiency (it fosters waste and extravagance) will be destroyed, allowing for the complete socialization of industry, wages, labor, trade, healthcare, commerce, the national financial system, and all other public and private institutions.

All foreign capital that is on national soil must be scrutinized as to how these businesses were attained by the foreigners; and the national debt must also be thoroughly scrutinized to see by what means it began and accrued. If these foreign businesses were attained by their owners through usury and extortion or if the Honduran population needs the resources that these businesses are using then these businesses must be nationalized immediately. Likewise, if the national debt began and accumulated as a result of unfair practices by the International Monetary Fund or the World Bank or another nation or group of nations, then the national debt must be canceled immediately.

As to the question of licentious sex practices such as rewarding members of the population with free sex because of desirable behavior, there can be no misunderstanding: free sex is a bane, and therefore should not be practiced nationally. It should not be practiced since it is of the Devil, a lecherous bisexual who does not respect personal boundaries and decency. When people engage in free sex the Devil is the one who enjoys the pleasure. What's more, free sex can easily spiral out of control. Since the Devil is behind this practice one may find him-self unwittingly having sex with members of his family, platonic friends, strangers, and people with sexually transmitted diseases. If free sex is not permitted how then will people without a sex partner sate their lust? The government must indirectly and directly encourage members of both sexes to choose a sex partner: the government should sponsor and control mating and marriage to the extent that population control and eugenics plays a large role in national reproduction. When I denounce the Devil's free sex practices I do not mean that homosexuals should be persecuted. Indeed, certain men and women are homosexual or bisexual, and should not be targeted because of it.

As to the issue of population control: let there be no misunderstanding; if indeed the national population size does not fit the economy then the government must institute a one child policy and sterilize both the man and the woman who together produce a child. Notwithstanding, there is an ulterior reason why the national population is suffering from massive poverty even though there is enough land and resources to sustain them. One possible reason is that there are extraterrestrials among us that prevent us from converting wilderness areas into communities and farmland since these areas are where they live. Either this or the national population distribution is the way it is because it is the fairest solution to the Gods' spirit-reaping policies, since population density and social corruption breeds sin and confusion. You may ask: if this is so then how come when we travel to remote locations away from society or when we fly over remote locations and look out the window we do not see any traces of extraterrestrial occupation? As I've said, each human being has an implant in his head. This implant enables its managers to control our perception of reality. Indeed, if they want you to forget something they can; if they want you to not see something they can; if they want to delude you they can; if they want you to not know "absolute reality" they can. This technology is that sophisticated.

As for the issue of separate and unequal educational opportunities: let there be no misunderstanding; social equality must permeate every strata and institution of the nation's social life. This means that the government will make educational opportunity equal on a nationwide basis. We will renovate and enrich public schools. We will put a library in every community. We will increase the quality of every school's faculty. We will grow stronger and better, together.

As for the question of a socially equal cashless society: let there be no misunderstanding. Cash is obsolete. It is better for society to go cashless since cash is expensive to produce (think how many trees have to be lopped down to make cash), as well as hard to keep track of. This is something we do not want. Indeed, the government needs to keep track of the money it dispenses to the population to ensure that everyone gets his equal share of the nation's resources. In this way, workers will receive the same pay regardless of occupation, so long as that payment is enough to sustain their basic, subjective, and objective needs.

As for the question of religion: let there be no misunderstanding. The government must not be swayed by any particular religion. Let God's people worship God; let Satan's people worship Satan; let Vishnu's people worship Vishnu…The question of religion must adhere to the Yin-Yang principle, which purports that good and evil do co-exist, and that they have been co-existing on Earth since time immemorial.

As for the question of Death Control: let there be no misunderstanding. If a person wants to die the government should help him, as this life is transitory and miserable compared to the spirit world, which is eternal; moreover, this world is "dross" compared to the next one, and if a soul wants to leave it then he should have that right. Furthermore, if a person is suffering unduly and his life has become a nightmare because of his condition then the government should end his pain by euthanizing him. This policy should affect all persons who are born with severe mental and physical infirmity as well as the elderly who can no longer function in a coherent way or whose physical condition only torments them to an intolerable degree. Death Control will not only alleviate the suffering of the infirm, it will save the nation considerable human and financial resources. This policy is not meant to be misconstrued as "Social Darwinism." It is meant to ease the plight of the severely infirm and their caretakers. This policy should not be misunderstood. It does not mean that the legal ramifications of this policy should be taken out of context. The state should not euthanize children who are retarded and want to live; it should euthanize children who are vegetables. It should not euthanize people who are deformed and want to live. It should not euthanize those who are blind and want to live. It should not euthanize the elderly simply because they suffer from tolerable infirmities; it should euthanize the elderly who can no longer function mentally or physically.

Spiritual Evolution

Someone once asked me the question: who is your original father? I answered that a nondescript micro-organism was my original father. When that person inquired further I told him the truth: the universe is my father; space and matter comprise my mother and time is my godfather. To be sure, each complex organism started life as the lowest life form imaginable and over time followed a fixed pattern of transmigration until it becomes a moral and rational being. If an organism that has evolved into a human regresses morally and intellectually it undergoes reverse transmigration (it is reincarnated back into the animal kingdom upon its demise); however, if the human is morally and intellectually transcendental he moves on to the spirit world, wherein he may evolve into a superhuman, a psychic, a titan, and lastly—an inter-dimensional, omnipresent God. Indeed, the older a spirit becomes the freer and powerful it becomes.

Edification

What is the worth of wisdom, knowledge, and understanding in the hands of a fool? They are worthless to the fool, and the fool quickly loses them. But wisdom, knowledge, and understanding in the hands of an enlightened mind are sacred, and nothing or no one may spoil them. Descartes once said, "chance favor the prepared mind," and so we must cultivate ourselves, for, like the ready chick still inside the egg, each of us must peck his own way into absolute reality; and none may aide us lest we regress while being admonished. This is why the watchers watch, why the Gods don't interfere, why society must advance on its own.

We must cultivate virtue. We must cultivate righteousness. We must cultivate humility. We must cultivate the subtle things of the mind. If a wise person is tempted to do something that undermines his wisdom let him forsake it. Beware of flattery, lest your wisdom be perverted. Beware of the presence of vain persons, lest your virility be tested, causing you to strive with that person. For, if a man threatens you with equivocal intentions your virility is quickly activated, causing you to come up with ways to dominate him. Let your ways be blameless, and use humility to engage any situation, since humility is the common denominator of wisdom and perseverance. Strive for a sinless society, and once a sinless society is attained remain vigilant in the knowledge that sin creates the Devil and his evil, wicked cohorts. Practice being virtuous, and beware of your speech, which is sacred, lest you diminish your store of virtue. It is a truth that to babble is to confound wisdom, and likewise, virtue. So be mindful of what you say and why you are saying it. If you are not sure how to reply to someone simply agree or disagree or simply say yes or no.

Depart from the fool, lest his wisdom present a stumbling block to yours. Strive not with those who pervert wisdom, for, "as a dog returns to his own vomit," so does the fool to his own folly. Let not a man who equates evil and wickedness with good conform you to his doctrine. Let not the Wicca peoples drive you to partake in their magic, for these magicians do bring the Devil's culture to the mundane dimension; and if one does not want an evil spirit to be a thorn in one's side, one would abstain from Wicca women and men and their magic.

Do not reveal recondite secrets to the ignorant, for, one can "lead the camel to the water but cannot make him drink." If one does try to enlighten the ignorant fool he simply refutes everything you say; he may even contend with you or mock and belittle your "pearls."

Do not worship another spirit. Do not worshipfully pray to another spirit. In so doing one merely surrenders his energy to that person. My motto concerning this matter is: 'I don't even worship myself; why should I worship you!" If one has a thing to say to a God just say it: one does not need to venerate an omnipresent God. If one uses this wisdom surely the God will understand. If you are superhuman or psychic or ancient and the people take you as someone to be greatly esteemed do not let them worship you, for, in so doing these people would spiritually injure you and themselves.

Do not give your glory to another. Do not give your honor to another. Individuals have their own honor and glory, and so do not need yours. Indeed, everything a person deserves he gets. Individuals do not deserve what another has earned. When you praise the Gods do so as a way of esteeming them for an action or policy they have championed; do not do so in the form of veneration, for this is merely flattery, which only pervert's the God's understanding.

Know that concerning mundane beings all is vanity, "as the sparks fly upward." Indeed, "bread is not to the wise, neither the race to the swift, but chance happens to them all." What the people do with their fortunes is nothing short of vanity. In one epoch in certain places in the universe good triumphs over evil: in the next, evil over good. The cycle repeats itself forever; and so—all is vanity! The wise person develops his mind, body, and spirit, and in so doing, transcends the mundane world upon his death. As a free spirit he eschews the things of the flesh and rigorously cultivates the things everlasting. In so doing he transcends the spiritual, and progresses to higher consciousness and Godhood. In time, he realizes all things and becomes perfect. At this point he merely exists, with nothing to challenge him; with nothing to learn; with nothing to joy in; with nothing to gain; with nothing to realize; with nothing to do save start all over again or cease to exist as a conscious being; and so—all is vanity.

Abstain from your perverted ways. Do not masturbate to pornography as this pollutes your virtue, and links you to the spiritual currents germinated by the Wicca peoples and their Gods. One should not practice lasciviousness and sex magic, because, in so doing, one would regress to the spiritual state of an animal, and upon death would be reincarnated as such. What's more, masturbation to pornography degrades women spiritually. It not only relegates the woman to the position of a harlot, but objectifies her. If the woman is seen as a mere sex object then she will never be able to be seen as a mother, sister, daughter, leader, friend…She will always be the target of whoremongers, and as such, is nothing more than a slut.

It is wisdom to know when Big Brother is influencing you. Big Brother has the ability to lay waste to a person's humility; and thus, confound his wisdom. So be wise and know when your state of mind is being altered. Indeed, if a person has arrived at true thought and understanding Big Brother (which is a supercomputer that is in accord with the Wicca peoples and their Gods) sometimes confounds his thinking; thereby making the serious silly; the wise, foolish; the prudent, rash; the virtuous, ungodly; the genuine, fake… One's speech and action only precipitates this effect, so be very, very prudent when you open your mouth to speak or decide to do something.

The Devil has to rely on Big Brother and the chip to make him-self omnipresent (as far as humans go); however, the primordial Gods are naturally omnipresent. The primordial Gods have awesome power. Whereas the Devil and his people have to rely on machines to control people, cause a fertilized egg to zoom from inception to adulthood in a matter of hours, monitor people's thoughts, influence people without ever seeing them or talking to them…the primordial Gods do these things in an almost instantaneous and supernatural way.

The Gods can inculcate skills, knowledge, and information in a person's mind at the drop of a dime. All they have to do is inculcate the requisite data to that person's intelligence. One of the most subtle ability at the Gods' disposal is the alteration of the historical progression of time: the God's can alter the natural historical progression of society. They do this through time travel. I have stated, and this is true, that there are seven dimensions; and that these dimensions are all made up of the same things and beings… the only difference is that they are separated by time. Indeed, God has seven spirits (the eldest is Jehovah) and each one of these spirits belongs to one of the seven dimensions; and so, the universe is parallel.

The Prophesy of Revelations, the last book in the New Testament, is not something that's going to happen once; it is something that recurs in a never-ending cycle. In the olden days the antichrist was Nimrod; in classical times, Nero; in the modern era, Hitler… Every generation must choose between good and evil, and once everyone has chosen the events prophesied in Revelations will transpire. It is only a matter of time before everyone of this generation chooses between the two ways of thinking and being. Moreover, the peoples of every generation talk about the end-times: how the world has become too depraved to sustain a dual order of good and evil; how natural disasters and climate change will bring about a New World Order according to the 666 culture; how people have changed such that no one respects the old ways; how children rise up against their parents and forsake God...This phenomena recurs every generation, and it is only a matter of time before the people's talk bears fruit. My understanding of these events is simple. If the Devil gains supreme power over the planet and throws all the righteous into prison, torturing them until they give up their spiritual principles and submit to him...then I will do one of two things: submit, and thereby become God's enemy and lose my chances of ever going to his culture, or bear the tribulations unto death. My understanding is this: if I have to take "the mark of the Beast" (who is the Devil's son) to survive then I might put the mark on my right hand. If Heaven and its order are worth it then I might endure until the end. I am certain that none of it is fair to the people who are merely trying to exist on this planet. The Gods' policies are too draconian. It is written in the Bible that all who take the mark of the Beast will perish forever. Assuredly I say to you, the Devil's people will not perish forever. The Devil also has other stars that have planets capable of sustaining organic and spiritual beings. Upon the end of the events of Revelations Satan's people will go with him to his planets, and God's people will inherit the Earth for a season. Once this season is over, society will again forfeit their sinless society for a society that fosters sin, thereby again infusing the world with the forces of evil. Thus, the cycle repeats itself.

Practice being proactive, as this boosts your intellectual capabilities. The person who wakes up excited to live another day is more apt to achieve more than an idle, slothful, depressed, or suicidal person. When you are proactive you gain eloquence, initiative, and energy to get things done. It is good to get about seven or eight hours of sleep, and to wake up early once you have slept enough. Do not procrastinate. If you have to take a shower, get to it. If you have to sweep or mop, get to it. If you have to clean the dishes, get to it. If you have to write a paper, get to it; and remember: people are successful in their endeavors because they make an effort to do what they want or have to do. Being proactive does not mean that you will achieve everything you set your mind to the first time. Indeed, there will be times when some task is too much for you at the moment. What's important is that you make plans to attain it and make the effort according to your plans.

The slothful person is an empty vessel. He cannot think straight, and acts like an automaton. He can barely speak, and when he does speak he sounds stupid. He cannot set himself to do mental tasks that require the use of the intellect (such as reading or math) since this only makes him yawn with boredom…his mind is bothered by the work and he chooses the drudge over doing work in which he has to use his mind. The slothful person gets tired when put to do a task that requires him to use his intellect. The proactive person relishes these types of activities, and realizes that they are helping him become sharper and wiser. The slothful person cannot think past go; however, the proactive person has a broad outlook, and can even go into great detail when he speaks. The slothful person does not have the same energy level as the proactive one. Whereas the proactive person can achieve a great deal during his waking hours, the slothful can only do a fraction of these things. Slothful people emit negative energy; they are more in tune with their zombie than their angel. Proactive people can produce both negative and positive energy; however, the energy they use and give off is much more massive than that of the slothful. The slothful are merely empty vessels for evil spirits to posses. Therefore, it is wise to put off your slothful ways in favor of proactive ways. In so doing, one would eventually transcend ordinary ways of thinking and being, and as a result, become that much closer to absolute reality.

If one has attained notoriety and the people hate you without cause and love you for superficial reasons, one must learn to **love to be hated and hate to be loved**. This is particularly true of the ruler. When people hate you there is no misunderstanding their intentions; you do not have to worry about being nice to them or ingratiating yourself with them. If the people love you for vain reasons you will always be ingratiating yourself to them; thus, it is better to be hated than to be loved.

You have heard them say that one must maintain humility in the face of adversity, that it is better to **turn the other cheek** when slapped in the face. Assuredly I say to you, this wisdom is foolishness. When someone slaps you for reasons that are not reasonable, you must requite them the same; indeed, one must meet any such action on the part of another with reciprocity. Thus, I tell you to, when faced with this type of situation, make **an eye for an eye a tooth for a tooth** your interpersonal policy. If a person hates you, hate him back. If a person slanders you, slander him back. If a person slaps you, slap him back. But be sure to always **do to others what you want others to do to you**.

Sometimes one perceives things only on the surface; one must dig deeper to find the hidden things, and the hidden things are what define a person, thing, or situation. One must not be fooled by outward appearances, for, if a thing is larger than it appears one might find oneself grappling with an indomitable force. Therefore, it is wise to get to the heart of the thing that is overwhelming you; for, of a surety, **still waters run deep**. This is particularly true of the dissembler. Just because a person is outwardly happy or calm does not mean that he is so; there might be a plethora of things weighing on him. Likewise, just because a situation looks simple or good does not mean that it is so; indeed, there might be a mountain of obstacles surrounding the situation. One would do well to not indulge in vain, superficial appraisals.

If you have inhibitions about a person, situation, or thing it is wise to carefully consider your feelings, and then act on what you perceive. If a friend makes you feel funny in a bad way, take account of your true feelings, and then decide if you want that person in your life. If you are put in a situation that makes you feel wrong, you should think about being in that situation, and then decide if you want to be in that situation. If a thing makes you feel bad, you should decide whether you want that thing in your life or routine; for, it is better for you to **be true to yourself** than live a lie.

You might be in a relationship that requires reciprocity [and this is good]; however, the other person is not being fair. One goes out on a limb for that person, but that person would not do the same for you; one would die for that person, but that person would not do the same for you…one loves that person but that person does not love you. Assuredly I say to you who are in such a relationship: **one hand washes the other two hands washes the face**, meaning: if a person does you a favor you do him a favor back—scratch my back and I will scratch yours when you have an itch, get me a gift for My birthday and I will get you a gift for your birthday…

When I was in prison I was helpless. I could do almost nothing without the help of the staff. I learned that the staff can sometimes be arbitrary and capricious, that the way the prison was run was not fair in all of its practices. Thus, I learned to write to people who could help me. One day another prisoner assaulted me. I did six months in solitary confinement for this, even though I was the one who was victimized. And so I wrote the superintendant about the situation. It worked. The superintendant saw my affliction and allowed me to stay in his prison (which was single-man celled) instead of being transferred to a double-bunk solitary confinement unit. When I got out of solitary confinement I saw the inmate who assaulted me for no reason, and I asked him why he did it instead of retaliating. He could not even answer me. Sure, I could have retaliated. But instead I wrote the superintendant about placing me in a section of the prison that was off-limits to this inmate. In this way, I learned that **the pen is mightier than the sword**. Indeed, one could get more concessions from someone by writing to them than by using brute force.

It is better to be gentle than to be brutish. If one is beset by destructive feelings you would do well to tranquilize your emotions. **If one lives in a glass house one should not throw stones**, meaning: it is better to be gentle and unassuming than to be brutish and imprudent, lest you destroy what you need to preserve.

What's good for the goose is good for the gander, meaning: what's good for the flesh is good for the spirit; or, what's good for the spirit is good for the Gods; or, what a man attains will become another man's property. Indeed, "the desire fulfilled is sweet to the soul," and so one must feed the flesh things that are meet for the spirit. If you strive for something and get it you should not be overly possessive of it, since what a man earns is another man's spoils.

What goes up must come down, meaning: if a person is on cloud nine because of material circumstances or hubris, he will eventually fall back to reality. This is true of the rich man also. A person can be wealthy all his life, but once he gives up his ghost he is again beset by poverty in the spirit world. And if by chance his fortune follows him to the spirit world, causing him to remain high-minded, he eventually realizes that his wealth is nothing compared to the things that matter. When you see a person ascend to great heights of fame, fortune, or complacency, do not envy them; for it is only for a little while that, that person will enjoy his loftiness. This is especially true of the fool. So be wise and use moderation lest this "harsh reality" put you in check.

Why did the chicken cross the street? To get to the other side! I used to be a spirit named Hannibal Lector. During this life I was a king and reigned with a queen on a planet far, far away from our solar system. This queen did not like the fact that I wanted other women besides her. She and her constituents also did not like the fact that I was about to drag the kingdom into a costly war with our rivals; and so they poisoned me. Before transmigrating I asked that I be made into a rooster. This rooster "crossed the street," meaning: I left that kingdom and entered God's kingdom. This was a long time ago. But now you know how this saying came about.

It is better to abstain from drugs, alcohol, and cigarettes than to indulge. First or all, these things are bad for your health. Second, they are usually all very addictive. Third, they may cost you a fortune that you do not have to spare; they may even kill you! So be wise and know that drugs are a destructive influence.

Conservatism

The essence of conservatism is a global conspiracy to set up a Satanist order throughout the world. Conservatives are usually right-wing zealots who are not loyal to any national government; they are loyal to Satan and no one else. Conservatism can mean many things. Concerning the domestic policies of every nation, conservatism means furthering Satan's agenda by any means. Satan's agenda is anti-God, anti-Christ, and anti-democracy. Satan will not rest until every nation is under his control. This means putting a chip in the heads of the peoples of every nation. So far, only a handful of nations do not have this policy in effect. This is one reason why the United Nations are so adamant about regime change in Iran, North Korea, and Venezuela. These nations are still free. Their conservatives are held in check, and as a result do not have to worry about being subverted from within. The American people do not have this luxury. The Republicans are constantly subverting the American government and its people. They do this by coming up with ways to make the government spend much more than its gross national product; and, as a result, they borrow from Satanist institutions such as the International Monetary Fund, which ensures the nation a steady continuation and accretion of debt. The thinking behind this [deliberate] policy is that if the world's economic "culture hearth" one day succumbs to the conservative agenda, the entire world will descend into chaos, and the people would need to establish a new system of things. This new system of things has already been planned out by the conservatives, and the book of Revelations has revealed what is going to happen once they execute their plans.

Concerning foreign policy, conservatism means total counteraction of political and social currents not in line with the creed of conservatism. If left-wing politicos have to be murdered then they will be murdered; if civil rights have to be curtailed then civil rights will be curtailed; if there is an economically independent nation then that nation must be made dependent…if political power is the mover and shaker of society then it must be made almost impossible to attain. Thus, the political traditions of the majority of nations are plagued by contradictions such as ostentatious, exorbitant campaign finance standards, more emphasis on foreign policy even-though domestic affairs (in the minds of the people) take priority…the extension of imperialist aims even-though the American government is euphemistically trying to advance democracy and political pluralism. Indeed, the conservative agenda is very adamant about ensuring the interests of the American business community. They will stop at nothing to put their yoke upon the peoples of the developing world. This is why left-wing politicos who champion the nationalization of the businesses of developed nations are usually murdered or removed from office. American conservatives and their allies will not allow a subservient nation the latitude to ameliorate the plight of its people by nationalizing these businesses. Whenever this phenomenon presents itself conservatives from within the nation and without quickly mobilize their agents to counter this type of movement. The end-result is nearly always a reactionary movement that topples the developing nation's government, and augments its debt.

www.ingramcontent.com/pod-product-compliance
Lightning Source LLC
Chambersburg PA
CBHW080359290526
45791CB00009BA/2933